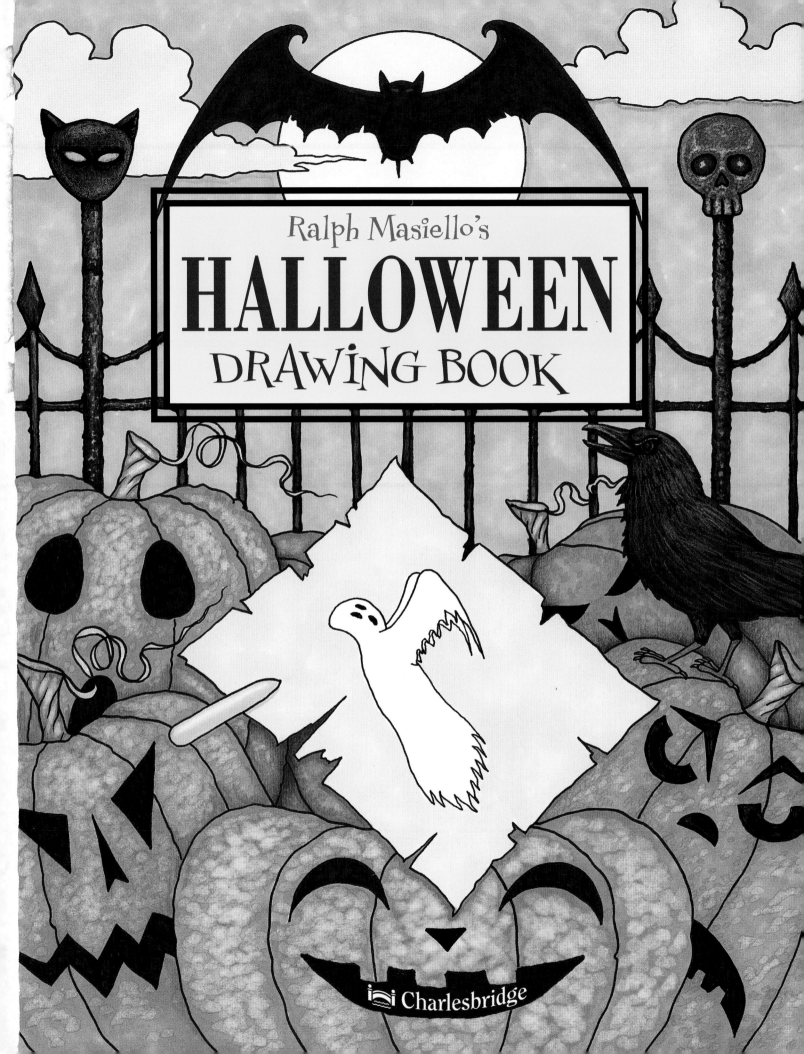

Ralph Masiello's

HALLOWEEN

DRAWING BOOK

Charlesbridge

To Zack, who loves drawing, and to all the ghoulishly great artists using this book—R. M.

Also in this series:
Ralph Masiello's Ancient Egypt Drawing Book
Ralph Masiello's Bug Drawing Book
Ralph Masiello's Dinosaur Drawing Book
Ralph Masiello's Dragon Drawing Book
Ralph Masiello's Farm Drawing Book
Ralph Masiello's Ocean Drawing Book
Ralph Masiello's Robot Drawing Book

Other books illustrated by Ralph Masiello:
The Dinosaur Alphabet Book
The Extinct Alphabet Book
The Flag We Love
The Frog Alphabet Book
The Icky Bug Alphabet Book
The Icky Bug Counting Book
The Mystic Phyles: Beasts
The Skull Alphabet Book
The Yucky Reptile Alphabet Book
Cuenta los insectos

Published by Charlesbridge
85 Main Street
Watertown, MA 02472
(617) 926-0329
www.charlesbridge.com

Library of Congress Cataloging-in-Publication Data
Masiello, Ralph.
Ralph Masiello's Halloween drawing book / Ralph Masiello.
    p. cm.
    ISBN 978-1-57091-541-3 (reinforced for library use)
    ISBN 978-1-57091-542-0 (softcover)
1. Halloween in art—Juvenile literature. 2. Drawing—Technique—Juvenile literature. I. Title. II. Title: Halloween drawing book.
NC825.H32M37 2012
743'.87—dc23   2011036736

Printed in China
(hc) 10 9 8 7 6 5 4 3 2 1
(sc) 10 9 8 7 6 5 4 3 2 1

Illustrations done in mixed media
Display type set in Couchlover, designed by Chank, Minneapolis, Minnesota; text type set in Goudy
Color separations by KHL Chroma Graphics, Singapore
Printed and bound February 2012 by Jade Productions in Heyuan, Guangdong, China
Production supervision by Brian G. Walker
Designed by Susan Mallory Sherman and Martha MacLeod Sikkema

Ghoulish Greetings, Fellow Artists.

Happy Halloween—my favorite holiday! Ever since I was a kid, I have loved the creativity, the drama, and yes, even the scariness of this spooky time of year.

In this book I will show you how to draw flying witches, dancing skeletons, and other creatures of the night. A haunted mansion and a creepy graveyard help set the scene for your monster mash.

Follow the steps in red to create spooky or just plain fun pictures. Try the extra challenge steps in blue to make your drawings even more bewitching. For an especially eerie effect, color in the negative space surrounding an object instead of the object itself. Fill in the object with black for a dramatic silhouette.

Have a frightfully fun time, and keep on drawing!

Ralph

Choose your tools

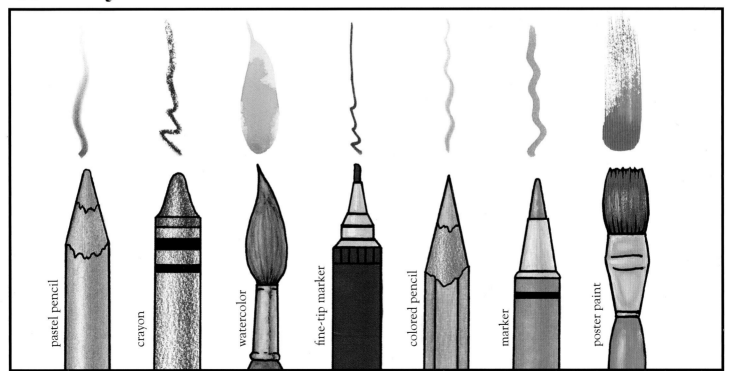

pastel pencil crayon watercolor fine-tip marker colored pencil marker poster paint

Pumpkins

Pumpkins can be tall, wide, round, lumpy, and lopsided.

Jack-o'-lanterns

These jack-o'-lanterns are really cutting-edge.

crayon

Bat

Add some holes or rips on wings.

Fill the night with winged creatures.

watercolor, marker, and poster paint

Ghosts

Happy, sad, or even mad—give your ghosts a face.

BOO-tiful ghosts!

watercolor and crayon

Black Cat

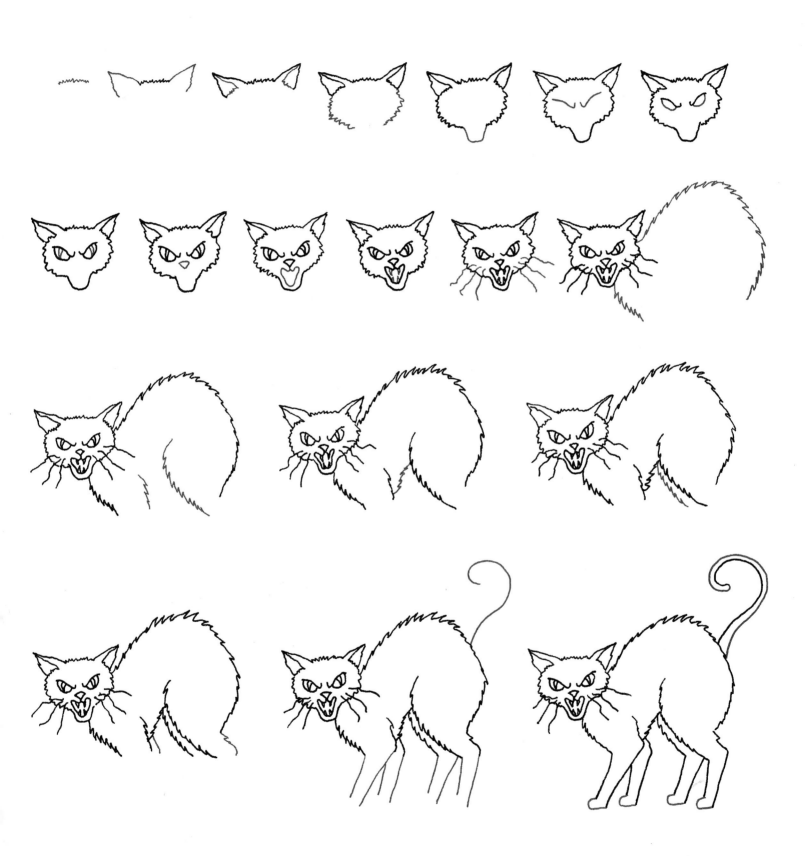

Purr-fectly creepy!

marker, colored pencil, and poster paint

Gravestones

Graveyard Fence

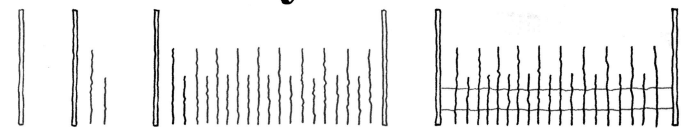

Leave it plain or add an arch if you wish.

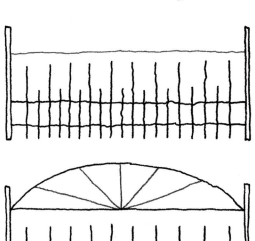

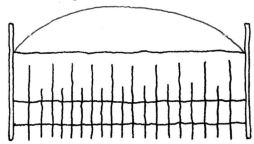

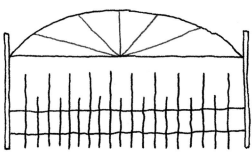

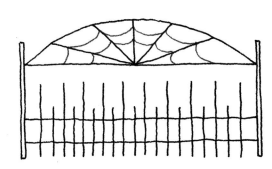

Fancy Finials

Fence Details

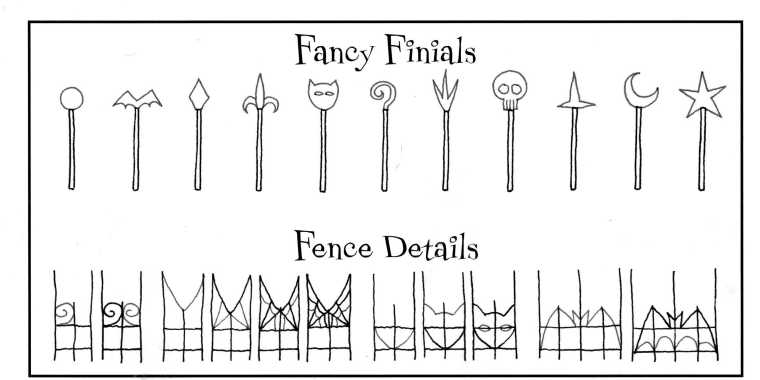

Enter the graveyard—if you dare!

Witch

A bewitching sight.

marker

Owl

Raven

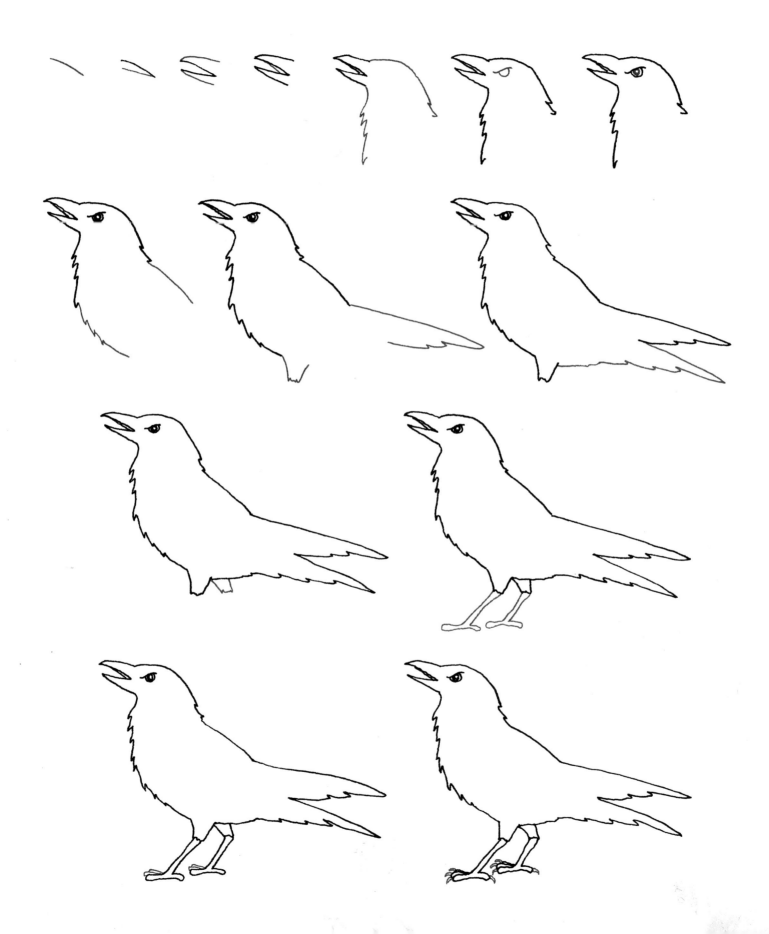

Scary Tree

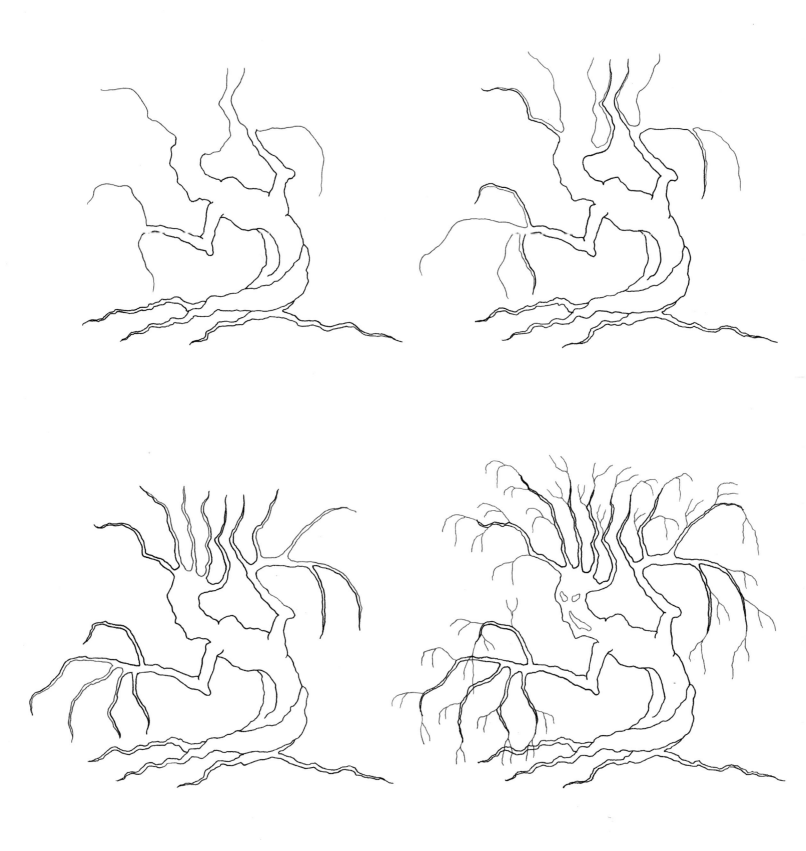

watercolor, marker, and colored pencil

Skeleton

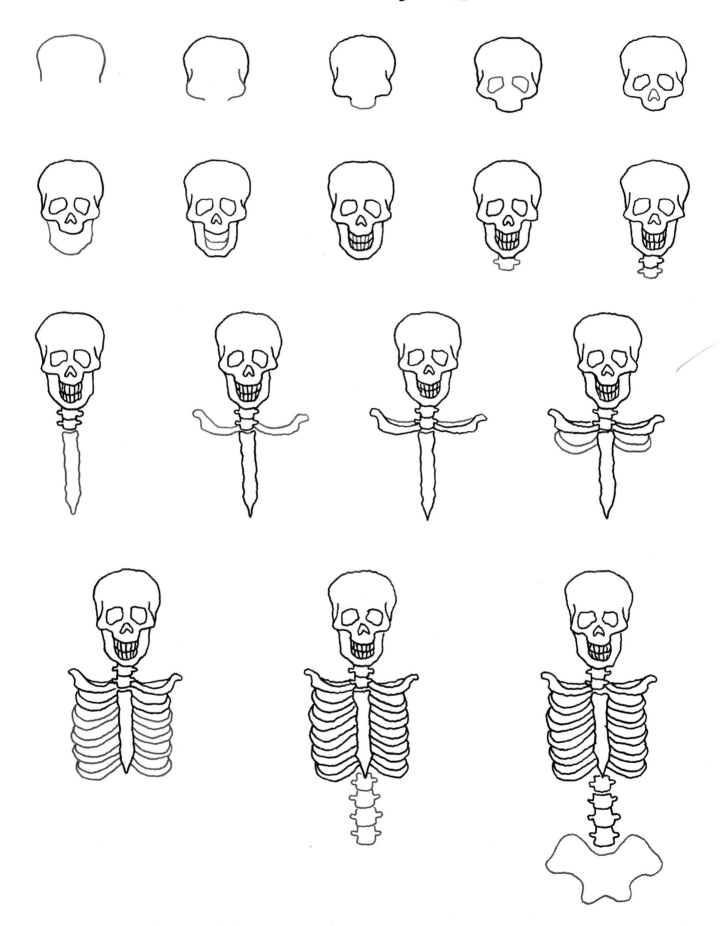

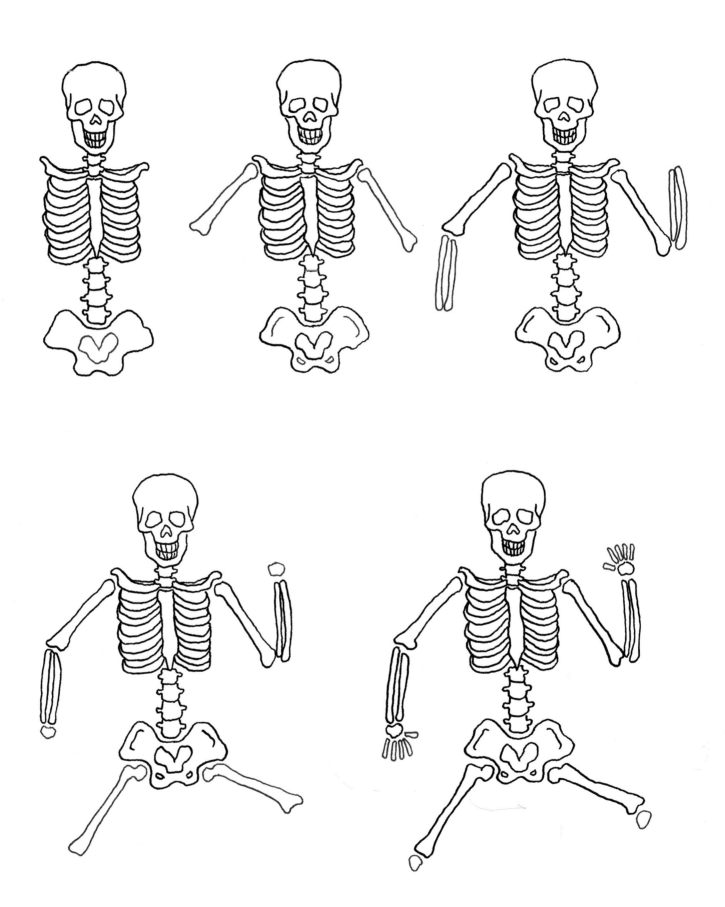

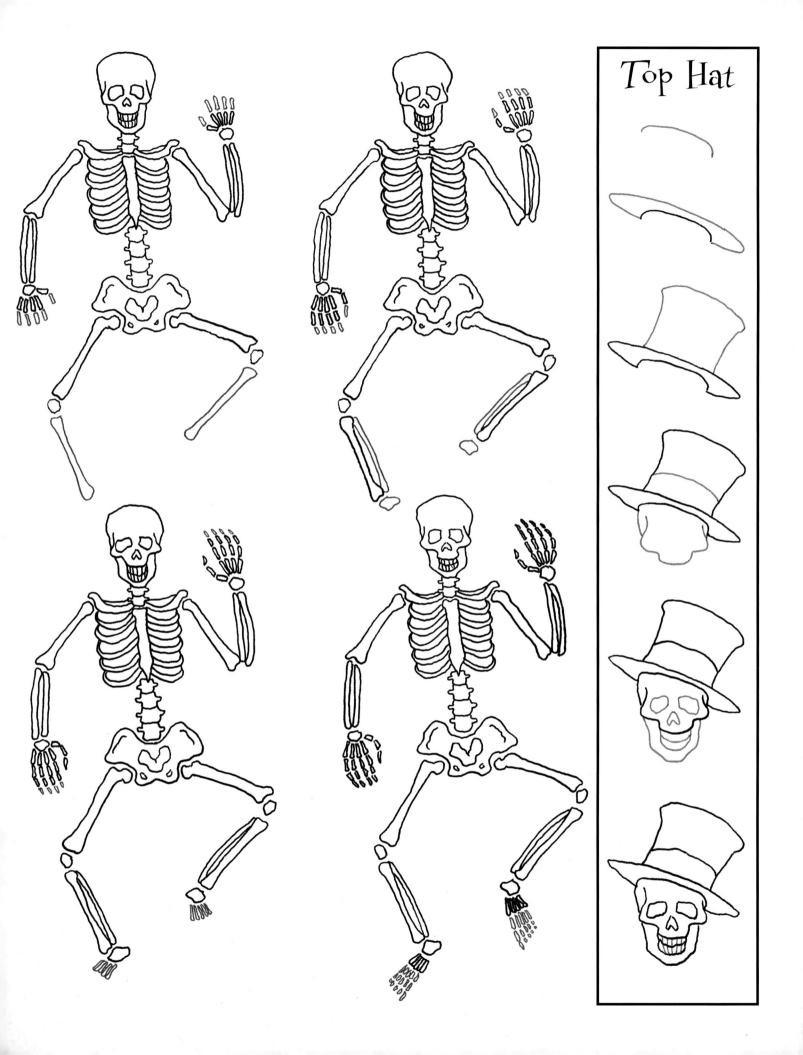

Top Hat

watercolor, marker, and colored pencil

Haunted Mansion

Have a very happy,
haunted Halloween!

Resources

If you're interested in reading some great Halloween stories or finding ways to make your Halloween party special, check out these spook-tacular books and websites!

Books

Baehr, Patricia. *Boo Cow*. Watertown, MA: Charlesbridge, 2010.
A pair of novice farmers encounters a ghostly cow that haunts their chicken farm.

Brenner, Tom. *And Then Comes Halloween*. Somerville, MA: Candlewick, 2009.
Join a neighborhood of kids as Halloween approaches and they prepare for an evening of trick-or-treating.

Bunting, Eve. *In the Haunted House*. New York: Clarion, 1990.
Follow the sneaker-clad footsteps of two curious characters as they tiptoe through a haunted house.

Evans, Cambria. *Bone Soup*. Boston: Houghton Mifflin, 2008.
A hungry skeleton talks a town of creatures into helping him make bone soup in this Halloween retelling of the classic "Stone Soup."

Farmer, Jacqueline. *Pumpkins*. Watertown, MA: Charlesbridge, 2004.
Discover fun facts about pumpkins, including history, growing tips, and recipes.

Stutson, Caroline. *By the Light of the Halloween Moon*. Tarrytown, NY: Marshall Cavendish, 1993.
A bumbling band of Halloween creatures wants to know who is tapping a tune in the dead of night.

Teague, Mark. *One Halloween Night*. New York: Scholastic, 1999.
Three friends discover their own magic one weird and wacky Halloween night.

Yolen, Jane. *Best Witches: Poems for Halloween*. New York: Putnam, 1989.
A clever collection of poems celebrates witch pizza (with extra poison ivy), witch fashion (basic black), the modern witch (who owns a condo), and more.

Websites

Websites can change. Try running a search for Halloween on your favorite search engine.

Big Pumpkins
http://www.bigpumpkins.com
Find out all about a huge hobby: growing giant pumpkins.

History.com: All Things Halloween
http://www.history.com/topics/halloween
Explore Halloween photo and video galleries, learn about the origins of the holiday, and print out carving patterns to try on your own jack-o'-lantern.

PBS Kids: Happy Halloween
http://pbskids.org/halloween
Share in the fun of the year's spookiest, silliest, and tastiest holiday with your favorite PBS characters.

Halloween Party Games
http://www.halloweengames101.com/halloween-games.html
Endless Halloween game ideas for your next party!

Disney Family Fun: Halloween Recipes
http://familyfun.go.com/halloween/halloween-recipes/
Make spooky treats like mini mummy pizzas or caramel apple monsters.